AUTUMN LIGHT

Carol Grever

ISBN: 978-81-19228-55-3

First Edition: 2023
Rs. 200/-

Cyberwit.net
HIG 45 Kaushambi Kunj, Kalindipuram
Allahabad - 211011 (U.P.) India
http://www.cyberwit.net
Tel: +(91) 9415091004
E-mail: info@cyberwit.net

Printed at Replika Press.

FOREWORD

Decades ago, with a new advanced degree from my Oregon graduate school, I accepted a position as an English Instructor at Phillips University, a small, private institution in Enid, Oklahoma. At Phillips, I taught two classes of Freshman English and a sophomore level course in British Literature. The freshman course included a unit in poetry. I consulted my major professor in Oregon for advice about a suitable textbook. Upon his recommendation, I chose *Sound and Sense, An Introduction to Poetry,* by Laurence Perrine. It was a good fit. I taught from it every term during my seven years at Phillips.

Perrine's text also informed my own writing. Teaching requires deeper digging into each topic, clearer understanding of each principle and poem. My current success and identity as a "poet" can be traced back to this early immersion in Laurence Perrine's basic textbook. I have now written and published seven books, two of which are collections of my poems. Perrine's explanation of the elements of poetry remains ingrained in my consciousness as a writer. *Sound and Sense* contains many of the world's best poems, both classic and modern. It still has a prominent place in my home bookcase.

Contents

A MAN NAMED EVE

A man named Eve
tosses long gray hair
adjusts his skirt
and leads the singing.
His hands pound piano,
bass voice recalls
songs of the past.
Aged listeners
hum the tunes,
sing some words,
smile at memories
of long-past youth.
No judgment here.
No question about
this man in ladies' dress.
The balm of music
envelops the room
suspends queries
takes everyone back
to youthful joy.

AFTER THE MOVE

This is my new place.
Black foothills underline
distant snowy peaks.
Sitting on the deck
I study dark vistas
hazy mountain views.
Uprooted after fifty years
loneliness pinches
though strangers are kind.
Smile out of habit
greet all I meet.
Walk by the creek
notice spring's green.
Open windows wide
breathe in fresh air.
Make the bed, feed the cat
sip coffee from my old mug.
Open a favorite book
familiar as a friend.
Not everything is foreign:
Lean into change,
create home.

ANNIVERSARY

I woke too early today,
winter sun on my face,
proclaiming an anniversary.
Two years have passed
since Mama let go,
relieved, I believe,
to escape pandemic flu
overcome confusion
rest her weary heart.
She lost her memory,
eroded years before.
Dementia's curse
sapped her vigor
erased her past
muddled her final days.
I vow to use this date,
and all my days to come
to honor and remember
Mother at her best.
Happy and wise,
dedicated wife
best ever parent:
My ideal in an apron.

ANOTHER CHANCE

Startled from my solitude by the
slam of something against my window
I see with sorrow
a female robin, reeling crazily
swooping sideways to the nearest branch.
She clings to the cottonwood
teeters, then flails blindly
to the bank below.
Blood runs down the glass.
The deck below is spattered with it.
Shocked by sudden violence
I'm wrenched by her pain.
She flops on her back
helpless in the dry grass.
She's broken.

Another flash of flight:
Her mate lands beside her
a flurry of feathers
surer than she
hopping, flying, circling all around.
He lands, decisive, on her struggling form
takes her flailing wing in his beak
and lifts her up
rights her into a nesting pose.
Stunned, she rests on the hillside
motionless with her wounds.
I watch, enthralled
The male waits,

protective sentinel.
She stays a long time.
Her restless partner leaves, returns
hovering with anxious attention.

She'll die, I think,
grieving innocent nature and
the cold hardness of my civilized glass.
The raccoons will take her tonight.
But resurrection recurs.
When next I look
the battered robin is *gone*
somehow escaped from certain death
safe, I hope, in her own nest.

Celebrating in cold twilight, I ponder—
Without her mate
would she, today, have died alone?

AUTUMN LIGHT

Cleaning four-o'clock beds is a rite.
Summer's end, nod to autumn.
Crackling dry leaves fall together
with etched mazelike designs,
each unique in its scarred demise.
There is a brilliance in fall light.
Ideas come whole
Like the last sweet raspberry
plucked by grimy gloves
from its sheltered place in the fence.
Aching poignancy of clear thought
burns with the flame of a maple.
Life is beautiful in autumn light:
Bittersweet, understood,
and short.

BANE OF AGE

"We retreat into the stillness of our own bones."

Kimberly Kralowek

Across the lunch table
he captures the space
in murmured monologue
I can't divert or avoid.
English words assemble
in aimless odd ways.
Moustache-muffled mumbles
die across the table.
Past and present collide,
mixed topics and tense
jumble into nonsense.
Soporific drone dulls senses.
Bored and trapped
I try to read his lips
nod silently, look down,
concentrate on my salad.
Will this meal never end?
I make an excuse and flee.
A walk in springtime air
calms frazzled mind,
makes this bane of age
feel almost bearable.

CAREGIVER'S PLIGHT

Accountable for all,
decades of decisions
weigh like coffins
in pall-bearers' hands.
Bearing the burden
layered stress builds,
covered by smiles
worn like a mask.
Fatigue takes its toll
through arduous nights.
In dim daylight
pick up the load.
May I say "I'm weary?"
May I wish for escape?
No! Keep moving,
dutiful day into night,
cost unseen
effort ignored.

COMFORTS

Comfort from a quiet night,
Kitty's soft purr at my side,
steaming coffee at daylight
my warm protection
from spring snow outside.
In the western distance
level plains reach high
to solid black foothills,
fresh snowy peaks beyond.
Grateful for comfort and plenty
happy with life as it is,
sing praise to a bountiful God
for this perfect Colorado day.

CORNERED SPACE

Both parents dead
first mate queer and gone
husband lost in dementia
sons in distant states—
one with invalid wife
one with bright new life.
Alone in my secluded place,
days confined to glimpses
seen dimly through a window.
The past is recalled,
what's next, unknown.
Wedged in the in-between,
I grope for meaning,
for anything I might offer
a fast-retreating world.
What if I'm useless,
my offerings ignored?
That question hangs
in my cornered space.

CREATIVE DISCOVERY

Inspiration slumbers
in an exhausted mind.
Tired ideas hide in shade.
My muse is not amused.
She sits aloof,
turns her gaze away
in growing gloom.
Even bright sun won't light
cloudy thought, worn words.
Better to rest awhile,
unjumble the mess.
Take a deep breath,
arouse creative mind!
With fresh vigor
awaken inspiration,
discover the poem.

DECEMBER SUN

Warm as springtime
on the westward deck,
mid-afternoon deception
fades in a chilling breeze,
ends with a shiver.
My inner winter
will never warm.
Old dreams failed,
sunny hopes departed.
Nowhere to hide,
the inevitable future
is forever frozen.

DIVIDED LIFE

Overwhelming need, sapped energy
heart asunder, caregiver dilemma.
Fatigue-drugged night traveler
blurs place. Here, or there?
Is she awake? Passing truck or
grumbling walker wheels on tile?
Short sleep, restless shifts, walking stupor.
Is this bed at home, or am I there?
Reach for grounding touch,
stretch slowly into today.
Open-eyed mountain sun
supplants dusty-draped dark.
Here, then there.
Daughter's duty, divided life.

(from my book, *Finding Home. © 2021*)

EMBUDO RIVER TWILIGHT

Sitting still in dying light,
nothing to do but watch,
I feel very small.
In this narrow canyon,
the river dashes downward,
altering its own path
in a mad April rush.
Thundering clamor
echoes on sandstone,
flying foam spatters rocks.
Currents twist deeper,
boulders roll below
as churning water
forces its own course.
Swimming in it now
would be impossible.
What if there's no choice?
Drawn into life's torrent,
desperate to stay afloat,
I fight for my life.
In the foaming torrent
push against rocky turns
avoid debris and tangled trees.
Deafened by river roar,
bruised and exhausted,
ignore my wounds,
claw up treacherous banks
scramble for safety.
Panting and spent

fall on bloodied knees,
grateful to survive.
For this battered victim
of an untamed river,
for this lone survivor
a lifetime flashes by.
Blind ambition fueled obsession.
Diving in with abandon,
fight to win every match.
Bravado welcoming challenge.
But muscles and minds tire.
Passing years erode ambition.
Dreams fade with fatigue,
drowned in toil and loss.
Year after year
confidence erodes.
Youthful plans modify
to unfulfilled hopes.
Like the roaring river
always eroding its banks,
passing years drown dreams.

FURRY NURSE

Snug under covers
heart to heart
warm fur against my chest,
Ellie hums her happy song.
Chosen from her litter
just weeks old,
she's grown mature.
Her unselfish warmth
comforts loneliness.
Few friends understand
Ellie Cat's sixth sense.
Her inner knowing
an uncanny power
to calm and heal.
She teaches courage
on dark nights,
purring of peace.

GHOST OF MY HUSBAND

Naked by the shaded window
he stands in muddled silence,
his confusion the wall between us.
"Are you cold? Hungry?" I ask.
Mute except for his repeated "No"
this ghost of my husband
responds like a child,
lost in the shadows of his mind.
I've learned not to insist.
Tactfully quiet, I try again,
lay shirt and slacks on the bed.
At last, declining underwear,
he pulls trousers over bare skin.
Still shoeless, he discovers
the parking lot outside,
as if he's never seen it before.
Like a bizarre horror film,
every detail in every day
is foreign, often fearsome.
What danger lurks in the hall outside?
It's safer, he thinks, to stay in bed.

GRANDMA'S QUILTS

Grandma sewed quilts
year after year.
Gnarled fingers
worked at night
till failing eyes
betrayed the craft.
Friendship quilts
had embroidered names,
sweet reminders
of youthful friends,
joyful times long gone.
Her hand-sewn wool
transformed scraps
of old men's suits
into warm beds,
restful memories
on winter nights.
Her quilts, her legacy—
comforting rest
blessed by family love.

GRIM IN-BETWEEN

Tail lights fading into twilight,
my red SUV driven away.
Mark of my independence,
that car no longer mine.
Beloved home sold,
possessions donated,
no business, no work,
no respected identity.
No urgent deadlines
except to stay alive
longer than my spouse,
longer than my little cat.
No fear of future till now:
Eyesight diminished,
dependent again,
this is my grim in-between.
Now my age is “old.”
Try saying, “I am old.”
It catches in my throat.
After this limited span
the next stop, the end.

GROUNDED

Foreboding forecast,
all flights delayed.
Planes line up, engines quiet.
Nothing moves on runways.
Schedules upended
plans interrupted,
nervous passengers
begin the anxious wait.
Apprehensive chatter
relieves some tension,
distracts strangers
as lightning streaks
threaten strikes.
Thunder crashes
rain pelts windows,
tension builds Inside.
Edgy as children
at home alone,
we watch and wonder.
Will we fly tonight?
Waiting is torture.

HAIKU FOR SPRING

Frozen water drops
diamond rainbows dancing
as I shift my gaze.

Pool-reflected sun
simmers colors of surprise
promises of spring.

Sleepy tabby cat
catches naps in warm sun
no fear of future.

Embroidered apron
folded in old cedar chest.
My mother has died.

Mid-summer thunder,
braced for tornadic winds
safe in dry shelter.

Springtime promises
fade in summer heat
melt into teardrops.

Bare feet on wet grass
summer's steamy treat
nature's cool massage.

Kitty's favorite perch
highest window in the house
her glimpse of summer.

Lazy Saturday
nothing pressing to do—
what woke me at dawn?

HOLIDAY PERSPECTIVE

Jolly Holly's a sham.
Shoppers race around
rush store to store
buy countless presents,
more than enough,
wasteful wrappings
crushed and stuffed.
Gathered families
forced to "be nice"
massive plates
filled up twice,
women in kitchens
faint with fatigue.
Confess this excess
Help those in need!
Christ taught us how.
Honor God's son
with a generous bow.

IN-BETWEEN

Morning to night
months flash past,
a confusion of time.
Day to day to day,
sameness settles.
Is it Monday? Friday?
What month? Year?
Seasons disappear
in a gray muddle.
Not ready to die?
Shake yourself awake!
Resolve to act!
Minutes count.
Boldly forge ahead
to discover your way.
Determined to live,
generate energy.
In-between is precious:
It is the gift of *now*.

LOCKED IN

Behind locked doors they sit, silent.
Blank faces shine in television's glare.
Old movies, shown each night,
keep memory care patients quiet.
Empty eyes stare at the screen.
Replayed films, forgotten overnight,
endlessly surprise this crowd.
Sitting close to hold his hand,
I wonder if he knows me,
his caregiver and wife,
sole connector to family life.
Does love exist in dementia?
Is desire gone forever?
Another day, another movie.
Hours turn to days, weeks, months.
How many are left for him,
for others locked in this half-light?
I grieve his death before it comes.

LONELY DRAMA

I repeat my lines
like an amateur actor
rehearsing a part.
Bits of lived history
whispered to myself,
quirky odd turns
crazy decisions
personal regrets—
melodrama too real
for polite company.
No audience here
for this nightly recital
in my solitary bed.
Only the cat hears.

MARCH 7, 2023

Two years have passed
since Mama let go,
happy to leave,
to join her only love
in forever's embrace.
Covid opened her door
to hoped-for heaven,
her escape from fear,
longing, isolation.
Theirs was a love
much admired
never ending.
In my dreams
joyous celebration
as they reunite.
My fond fantasy—
a blissful reunion
to last forever.

MEMORABLE POEMS

Poems defy description,
each one unique.
A poet presents
unmarked doors
flung open wide.
Behind those doors,
startling truths
shadowed or bright,
a defiant toad
or bluebird in flight.
Poems cheer hearts
nourish minds.
Uplifted in verse,
dark-cloud storms
yield to sunshine.
Inspiring poems
stir imagination
with lavish grace.

MEMORY BOOK

Photos of fun enrich old age.
In meditative moments,
recover youthful joys
evoke the daring past.
Red canyon walls frame the sky,
Gunnison River laps the shore.
Canoes in a line run rapids.
Bikes on wild adventures
explore foreign horizons
new mountains to climb.
Overseas tours entice
but home is always best.
Views from Green Mountain,
our Boulder nest below,
busy kitchen, springtime sun,
promise of new gardens.
Passing years slow our pace,
major moves, painful loss.
A narrower prospect
frames these days.
But the center still holds.
Resolve to carry on.
Turning precious pages,
my memory book brings peace.

MISSING MY MOUNTAINS

Rocky Mountains' east wall
towers above south Boulder.
Aptly called "The Flatirons"
enormous sandstone cliffs
shaped like old-time irons,
an imposing backdrop
for our snug little home.
My morning view
below the monoliths,
golden in the rising sun,
blessed twenty years.
That welcome sight
inspired many poems.
Then we moved away.
Now viewed from afar
those foothills merge,
seem a solid black base
for snowcaps beyond.
Lonely and homesick,
I miss my Flatirons—
now too far away,
symbols of a loving past.

MY LITTLE BOY

Holding his limp hand,
I walk more slowly now.
His steps are hesitant,
feet shuffle along—
no hint of former zest
on his unforeseen path.
Thinning hair, dim eyes,
deeply wrinkled face
reveal an aged child,
loved as a husband,
now like a little boy.
Maternal instincts prevail
frustrate desire, deepen loss.
Which is worse?
To be the pitied elder,
or the weary carer?
Only time can bring
an uncertain guess.

NAME YOUR LOSSES

I am alone, I am lonely.
I had a husband,
he doesn't know me.
I have two sons
with separate lives.
I had a car
I couldn't drive.
Had many friends
but I moved away.
I had a home
sold when I left.
Most painful loss
is eyesight.
Alone in my own body,
too many losses.
Looming challenge:
Accept reality.
I'll do it: I must.

NIGHTLY REHEARSAL

Stories under the covers
whispered softly to myself,
prepare my daylight lies.
Nighttime visions
forge brave accounts—
wistful fabrications
I hope to believe.
In morning sunshine,
cheerful smiling wit
feigns contentment.
Look more closely!
Tested by candid truth,
rehearsed stories fail
in reality's harsh light.

NINTH DEATHS

Ninth deaths
are hard to recognize.
Rare cats play dead
sometimes
then Phoenix-like
rise and rise again
from cool ashes to warmth.
My cat seemed dead—
beaten, bitter,
looking life-lost.
But he rose.
And now I wonder:
Was his last death
his eighth?
How many more to go?

NOTES IN THE NIGHT

Always, forever!
That was our promise
practiced for decades.
Alzheimer's mind theft
required our parting.
Faint echo of himself,
my infirm mate
now a quiet child.
Bodies separated,
lovers no longer,
I care for him still
more mother than wife.
His illness terminal,
I grieve in advance,
dread widowhood.
Awake on solitary nights,
vows honored still,
"Always" is my pledge,
"Forever" so long.

OMEN OF DESPAIR

My husband Is gone.
Only blank gaze remains.
Engaging smile erased,
diminished body weak.
Solitary confinement
in the cruel prison
of his own mind.
Locked in memory care
he languishes in silence.
My painful daily visits
measure loss after loss.

I grieve his death

before it comes,
my relentless façade
an omen of despair.

PATCH-WORD QUILT

Wakeful dreams tease,
raise rare possibilities.
Sleepless musing
creates my fantasy quilt.
Its images recall the past.
Remembered emotion
gathers artful colors,
awakens imagination.
Key words evoke events,
enliven every patch.
Word after word appears,
inspires evolving design.
Calm to alarming,
gaudy to grim,
diverse patches emerge,
probing the past.
As morning breaks,
sunlit squares hearten
offer comforting warmth,
uplift the new day.

PIECE-MAKERS

Our world is broken.
Separated fragments
abandoned in chaos
scatter randomly
like gamblers' dice.
Fragments of lives
shatter in confusion
memories twisted
future feared.
Can courage remain
to heal this ruin?
Only Piece-Makers
can salvage hope.
Piece-Makers
pick up the scraps,
transform splinters
into renewed lives.
Love is the remedy
for broken spirits.
Kindness is the balm
to treat despair.
Gathering the wounded
with genuine care,
these healers at heart
preserve sanity
rescue the lost.

POEM SEED

"We are the womb of possibility."

The minister's comment
shines in memory,
awakens imagination
invites fantasy.
What wonders await
ripe with promise?
Miracles may emerge,
brilliant creations
to challenge doubt,
aid a weary world.
But birthing is hard,
the process so painful
only the strong endure.
Nurture the seed,
claim the prize!
Write your poem.

PRAYER FOR PEACE

Waking nightmares
plague the world.
Children, shelled in war
bleed on blasted streets.
Lifeless bodies sprawl,
heaped together
unnamed, unburied.
Slaughtered women
hold dead babies,
victims of Putin's madness.
I pray to God,
who surely listens:
"Let the wars end!
Let the babies live!
Let the world breathe,
finally sane and free!"

RAVISHED

Poem for the Pandemic

Epidemic attacks
unhinge the world.
Vicious viral rapes
drive lethal shudders.
Ambiguous pause
brings hopeful suspense.
Fatalities slow,
panic subsides.
But this mindless predator
doesn't relent,
assaults more victims
with deadly peaks,
ravishes the world.
Will its rippling climax
birth fearful offspring?
What churlish bastard
will its issue be?
That answer hangs
in poisoned air.

RECLAMATION

A bushel of apples
fresh from our tree
shine shyly in the basket,
fragrant red promises
of winter pies to come.
Knife sharpened
quarter the first apple
inhale the aroma of
firm fruit inside.
Organic apples
sometimes disappoint,
blighted at the core.
Outer impressions
often mislead.
Some are perfect—
crisp and tart,
others host worms
lurking undetected,
black mold inside.
Looks do deceive.
All have bruises
all need work
but are mostly good.
It's natural.
Spots of rot aren't fatal.
Slicing up the lot
from a whole bushel
few are hopelessly lost.
A sharp paring knife

saves useful scraps
cuts away blemishes
salvages the best.
With spots removed
remaining fruit is sweet
wholesome, sustaining.
Like us, good outweighs bad.
Savory pies come from
valued parts of flawed apples.

RELUCTANT RECOGNITION

He's already far away.
I must close my eyes
to picture my mate
fondly recalled,
gradually replaced
by an elderly child.
Resigned hours on end,
he gazes in silence,
furrowed face
ashen in fading light.
Exhausted and weak
eyes and memory blank,
mood uncertain as his gait,
he fades in quiet confusion.
Spousal duty honored,
my visits to Memory Care
frustrate passion,
magnify harsh truth:
Marriage is replaced,
parenthood repeated.

RIGHT TURN

Rocky Mountain forest
evergreen perfume,
rain on a metal roof
stirs verdant memories:
Science Camp summer.
My insane decision—
volunteer as camp cook.
Seven-day weeks,
three meals daily,
famished students
need tons of food.
Voracious appetites
fuel adventure.
My nine-year-old
romped in the river
breathed open air
explored the forest
thrived in freedom.
I hiked to privacy
journaled my truth
discovered love.
That summer of liberty
changed everything.
It was a right turn:
flatlander no longer,
mountain dweller for life.

SCARS OF SCARCITY

Ragged tops of faded socks
peek under tired jeans.
Soiled pink sweatshirt
re-worn for a week,
dreary old clothes prevail.
Better outfits, kept "for good"
hang unworn, out of style.
Stale re-heated coffee,
dabs of left-overs pack
freezers and fridge,
pantry shelves weighted
with outdated cans,
food saved for years
ravaged by time.
Crippled car, new in '92
clutters the bulging garage.
Vinyl records warp in stacks
by a silent broken stereo.
Unused parlor a musty museum,
Victorian furniture
visible history of a long life.
Multiples of everything
crowd closets and drawers.
Save it all, wrecked or whole.
Great Depression mindset
stores and hoards.
Detritus collects
in a stagnant pond.
Scars of scarcity
linger for life.

SHADOW MAN

He's safe, I guess,
wandering halls,
no destination.
He's confused,
not unhappy,
one long moment
after another,
simply existing.
Years in memory care
will never cure.
When music offers
welcome excitement
brief joy grows.
Piano or harp,
accordion or horn,
any performance
offers innocent bliss.
Drawn, childlike
to a live show
he may dance
his awkward jig
to find the fun.

Ice cream delights,
other food bores.
He's more child
than vivid man.
He still knows me,
but bereft of desire.

Night follows day
in numbing sameness.
He's gone—
only his shadow left.

SOUNDS OF "PROGRESS"

Sites for new homes,
acres of farmland
targeted for "progress."
Crawling monsters,
insistent BEEPS
scatter silence
shatter sanity.
Flattened fields
transform with traffic,
tractors and trucks
scream disruption.
Incessant noise
clears this ground
expels peace
erases the past.
After construction
hundreds of townhomes
will cover these fields.
They call it progress.
Will their new sounds
feel gentler?
That question lingers.

STORIES UNDER THE COVERS

Stories under the covers,
whispered softly to myself—
fabrications I believe,
or hope to.
Like children's fiction
I forge brave accounts,
rehearse my daytime lies.
Living in community
with practiced smiles
I affect unfelt warmth,
project boldness
with habitual chat.
Boisterous wit
mimics happiness,
feigns strength,
hides silent grief.
Despite my lies
daily demands crush
my bedtime stories
in reality's harsh truth.

STRESS, OR DEMENTIA?

"I don't remember."
No matter the topic
I keep saying that.
My friend shakes her head,
advises memory tests.
I say, "It's only stress!"
Secretly wondering,
self-doubt rules.
If I lose my mind,
I would rather die.
Thankful for a good life,
lived on my terms
it could end on my terms.
Test the question
wait a bit, then decide.
Determine the conclusion.

TALKING TO MYSELF

When the lights go out,
darkness shelters
dimly mirrored frowns.
I dare to utter aloud
words that plague me
hidden in daylight mind.
Thoughts tumble out,
a waking nightmare
cried aloud under covers.
"Trapped! I'm trapped.
This wasn't my plan!"
Night after night
turning to months.
Can it be a year?
No horizon of hope,
no escape in sight.
"I will die here—just here."

TWILIGHT INSIGHT

Memorize this sunset:
Bright rose and gold
glow on ebbing clouds.
Dusky low foothills
reach for the gentle light
as evening softly settles
on the waiting plain.
Twilight quickly fades
like these last years.
Days and lifetimes end
in such silent darkness.
Another day passed,
less time to consider
what it all meant,
whether it mattered,
what is yet undone,
what will be left behind.
Imminent night
may suggest answers
or simply end the light.

WASH MY SOUL

May you be held in compassion.
May your pain and sorrow be eased.
May your heart be at peace.
—Buddhist Blessing

Alzheimer's stealth
erases my mate.
Stages of grief:
Shock of discovery
futile disbelief
heartfelt regret
relentless ache.
More loss in sight,
rising dread!
Consoled by friends,
held in compassion,
I shall live on.
Sustained by prayer,
faith-filled tears
wash my soul.

WHEEL SPINNING

Round and round,
repeating circles
day in and out,
in dazing haze.
Stupor of boredom
no thrill or delight,
months into years
lost with no fight.
Wake up your mind
with reckless glee!
Forgo permission
get wild, get free!
Grab bites of life
with no sorry strife.
As wild circles slow
memories will glow.

WINTER HAIKU

shrine candle flickers
stuttering light shimmers, grows
inspiration lives

bare locust branches
stark patterns on pale March sky
tenderest black lace

crystal mountaintops
point skyward, float between
snow-clad clouds and fog

old snow holds hostage
glassy ice peaks in March
gold in morning sun

snow veils frigid dawn
migrating blackbirds practice
dawn's raucous chorus

flurries ride wind waves
springtime whitewash here, then gone
iced sun, patient, waits

bleak cold before dawn
grey turning rose, then gold
warming sun the artist

WORDSMITH

A compelling calling:
Shape thoughts
Inspire actions
Stir with words.

Gentle words soothe hurts,
tender words express love
recall sweet memories,
awaken erotic passion.

Words can change minds
bring healing or hatred,
evoke laughter or tears
sadness or comfort.

A wordsmith wields
powerful tools
that impact lives,
transform the world.

WRITER'S IMPASSE

Walls of isolation
smother inspiration.
Lonely seclusion
fails to excite
weakens energy
saps motivation
silences poetry.
Idle minds decline
bereft of fresh air.
Fighting for breath
in empty space,
creativity wanes
imagination withers.
Possibilities die
with no original words.
Nothing left to say.

WRITING MY ELEGY

Writing in twilight
requires resolve,
tests determination.
Stumbling blind,
fearful of what's next.
Too soon to panic
but age affirms
my ending looms.
Running on empty,
time is short.
Passing days
failing light
growing dread.
Gloom deepens.
Weigh prospects,
pray for guidance
long for foresight.
How many days left
to write my elegy?

www.ingramcontent.com/pod-product-compliance
Lightning Source LLC
Chambersburg PA
CBHW022203160726
48282CB00024B/304
* 9 7 8 8 1 1 9 2 2 8 5 5 3 *